THE THIRD BOOK OF APHORISMS

NATHAN FREEMAN

To order additional copies of this book, contact:
Xlibris
1-888-795-4274
www.Xlibris.com
Orders@Xlibris.com
538182

DEDICATION

To Thomas, Kevin, Ollie and the Williams,
from whom I learned that there is much truth
in dialogue and even more in friendship.

APOLOGIA

To even begin to write a preface for this sort of work, is to give away too much of its secrets. So instead of giving easy hints to the reader, I will first explain how the book came about. Truth be told, the *real* third book of aphorisms is entirely lost. It was an opus of rare genius and delicate, yet profound thought, the likes of which the world will not see again in the near future. Sadly, that book was left behind in some beer hall at the Munich Oktoberfest, and has never been seen since. What stands before you is the attempt at recapturing some of that genius of what was lost, because to make an attempt and fail is better than no attempt at all.

Being the *third* book of aphorisms implies there are in fact two other earlier books. This idea finds itself to be in close accord with the reality, but as of now I see fit to maintain these earlier works in my private manuscript collection as too much the "wild and wandering cries, confusions of a wasted youth." Perhaps if random whimsy change my mind, and the public demand it strongly enough, these too will see the light of day in the form of a published book.

Finally, though I do not want to give anything more away than I already have—that would take the joy, and "fun" out of getting at the meaning of these aphorisms, I will say one thing. Please read these following words very carefully. Read thoughtfully, and try to realize that to disagree is to begin a dialogue that ought to lead toward some deeper understanding of self and the world. Most of all, though it might be too much to ask your charitable thoughts regarding mine, at least endeavor to read with a certain amount of indulgence and know that these aphorisms are in fact not nearly as extreme as they might appear at first glance.

Chronologically this book was more or less written before the *Tractatus de Societate* and in many ways can be read as a prelude to that book. The two are certainly capable of shedding light on each other, while remaining autonomous in their own right.

Finally I would like to personally thank (in writing) Melissa Spilman for her help in editing the manuscript and for her artistic genius as displayed on the book cover, and Isabel Bleckmann for some suggestions at getting my German closer to the *Rechtschreibung* standards currently in use. I admit to having maintained several out-moded ways of rendering the German as I thought it got at the meaning more nearly than the new rules of style.

THE THIRD BOOK OF APHORISMS

1.
Starting a new book is to make a new beginning—whether
reading or writing, one full of hope and excitement,
for no one knows how the story will end.

2.
Truth is never lost, only on occasion forgotten for a while.

3.
It is said that Life is fragile; this is quite true. On the other hand, there
is no power stronger, more dynamic, or sophisticated than Life.

4.
"Someday, perhaps, I will find you once again"—this sentiment keeps
the hope of many alive, and to hope is remain among the living.

5.
For these once-great men, not only their lives and deeds are obscure, but
the very names themselves. Does this in fact diminish their greatness?

6.
Falsehood is always self-destructive; perhaps not
immediately, and certainly not apparently.

7.
I refuse to submit to the yoke of dehumanizing experts.
Though they kill me, at least by death I will have preserved
something they can never understand: *Humanitas.*

8.
Never shun or avoid the danger of human passions
for the safety of etherized, sub-human apathy.

9.

Is it nobler to die for the sake of ideas or persons? Who is higher Socrates or Christ? (Nietzsche, it seems, cared for neither of these two.)

10.

No one has ever been truly great, who was
also not their own greatest critic.

11.

Never let anyone drink you under the table, until you are under the table.

12.

How often has greatness passed through our midst, and yet
due to our weakness and fear, we did not recognize it!

13.

Even the apparatus of contemporary society lends itself to the
banal. How much less serious is the auto than the horse, the light
bulb than the candle, the email than the hand-written letter!

14.

If even our delusions are more beautiful than "reality"
today, that is simply more evidence for the falsity
of this reality we have made for ourselves.

15.

How in fact can "reality" be less-real now than before? This seems,
and perhaps is a contradiction, but yet that is exactly how it feels.

16.

Being sad serves no evolutionary purpose; that is why
I like it. It makes me feel all the more human.

17.

The difference between having sex and making love is
comparable to the lightning bug and the lightning.

18.
Had too much, or too often, any powerful pleasure
diminishes so much so as to cease being pleasure at all—
so obvious yet so unheeded in the present age.

19.
The contemporary man does not ask what *is*, he only asks what is next.

20.
Those who treat other humans as mere means
have lost their humanity only slightly more than
those who enjoy being treated as a means.

21.
"Effectiveness" is the least human, the least true, and least worthy
category on a scale of determining true value of the thing.

22.
There is no joy or excitement comparable to that of going
home. What then of those who have no home?

23.
The Protestants, by making every man a "priest," increased,
perhaps, the religious devotion among themselves in general,
but also created peoples obsessed with religion to the neglect
of culture. This is why, historically, in Protestant countries it
was the irreligious and non-dogmatist who became the creator
of culture (cf. Goethe and Keats). Since culture drives human
society, secularization was the inevitable result. Religious
devotion led to its own self-destruction in this instance.

24.
Constant "busy-ness" is the attempt at feeling important, as
diversion is to the attempt at true joy. Both the former terms
are ultimately unsatisfying but are rather ways of remaining
distracted from the true reality and from truly living.

25.

Natural Law is the means by which reasonable men may live together peaceably, prosperously and even joyfully. Many pagan civilizations have done fairly well for themselves only by virtue of following Natural Law, because reason is a natural virtue available to all men. However, in the absence of reason, there is no understanding of Natural Law and barbarism ensues. By denying Natural Law the contemporaries have created a situation, though full of technological "progress," rife with moral and aesthetic barbarity. It is a situation ripe for the destruction of their so-called civilization.

26.

We cannot and should not return to a pre-existentialist worldview. Their critiques and sentiments regarding Enlightenment-style reason and modernism were valid in many ways. Today, Truth can be found only by going through and *beyond* Nietzsche.

27.

How are we supposed to fathom the glory of God, who is a person, without persons on this earth who mirror that glory? We could look into the starry heavens but these are too impersonal. We could look to our great men, but we have none . . .

28.

Sins committed due to idleness, though often the least heinous outwardly, are often the most dehumanizing because they lack passion, require no force of will and have the unanimated quality of boredom. They deaden the soul by making it small.

29.

Living with oneself is perhaps the only thing harder than living with someone else.

30.

It may be true that the fittest survive, but when it comes to the human race "fitness" must be defined to include so many more important factors than mere genetics and physiology.

31.

Every ideological movement that is successful in superseding the old order of things then goes on to define its own "classics" which become the pillars of a new order. The once creative movement ends up like the old—static. It is like the revolutionary who becomes a tyrant in his own right after toppling the king, inviting the next revolution.

32.

Adopting a new theoretical or theological perspective can sometimes simply be an excuse to follow another course of action previously desired. The worshippers of Bacchus had a religious ground to get drunk and have orgies. This does not make that worship necessarily false, but it does make it questionable.

33.

The fleeting nature of all things is only grounds for despair and melancholy when it comes to the beautiful things which we would like to last forever: Love, Truth, Life.

34.

The vocation of teaching serves two primary purposes: to make known truth and to preserve culture. We, in the present age, no longer believe in truth, and we have only paltry remnants of culture. Yet for some reason we still have teachers. The momentum of vast organized systems is not to be under-rated, like a rotting corpse produces heat and stench though the life principle be gone from within it.

35.

There is a reason that Schumann titled that little piano piece "The Happy Farmer." The farmer is happy because though his work be often arduous, he at least enjoys knowing that his labors were worth the while. Few in the modern age can feel thus about their works and days.

36.

Forcing love is like forcing a poem; it is not to be done. Even if there is a mastery of technique, without spirit, none may attempt it without seeming a fake.

37.

No human is so important as to be essential in holding
the universe together. None is so worthless as to be
superfluous once gone. This should tell us precisely how
much we are, or are not, to hold onto our own life.

38.

It would seem impossible to miss someone you have never met. Yet
I miss Nietzsche, Thomas Merton and Diamond as much as I miss
anyone. Perhaps "miss" is not the right word: I long for them.

39.

It is only after mastering the classics that one can go on to truly
great works of creativity. Human creativity stagnates when there
is no foundation to build upon or react against and thus the blasé
and pedestrian nature of "culture" in the present age. Neither do we
stand upon the shoulders of giants, nor do we tilt against them.

40.

Most everything looks at least half decent when new. The key is to make
something that will still be beautiful when it reaches a state of ruins.

41.

"Nothing German is feminine, not even their females"—
the observation (and advice?) of a good friend.

42.

To eliminate all risk and danger in life is to destroy our very humanity.

43.

He who follows only his feelings remains forever a child.

44.

Hope is the opposite of stoic resignation, though
outwardly they are often indistinguishable.

45.

"I may have lost, but I am not defeated; and shall
never be, for defeat is merely a state of mind."

46.
Life is an adventure, and if not, then that is your own fault.

47.
"If you do not understand the profundity of my truth it is your own deficiency." What arrogance! Yet often this is in fact the case.

48.
What did deep thinkers do before the advent of pen and paper? They spoke to actual humans *in vivo* and if they were quite good we remember both their names and teachings—Socrates, Buddha, the Christ.

49.
These days a hearty nationalism is acceptable and admirable for all those who are neither European nor Japanese. There is little logic to the standards of our cultural perceptions.

50.
Is it better to do well or to do poorly at a task that is inherently degrading and insipid?

51.
"Tomorrow, I am going to kill myself"—we always put off the greatest of our actions to another day.

52.
I defy and conquer all those who would put me in a box; I refuse to be dissected.

53.
German Idealism gave rise to the modern university because only by having general concepts, generally acknowledged, can intense scholarly research be fruitful. For by being circumscribed those ideas become worthwhile and intelligible. The breakdown of that Idealism meant the inevitable breakdown of the university, as such, for now nothing is broadly intelligible to either specialist or non-specialist.

54.

To be un-refined, unintelligent and uneducated—these are
certainly no great sins; neither are they grounds for great pride.

55.

It is difficult to say in which estate men are more miserable: when
they have to work like dogs, seemingly to no end, without a moment
to reflect; or, when they have so much leisure as to experience
the ennui and meaninglessness of endless decadent diversions.

56.

"If you are not having a good time, you are not drinking fast enough."

57.

I wonder if the Puritans truly loved God, or if in their
fear, they secretly hated him. Of course in that case it
is rather nice to be among the elect regardless.

58.

"One thing is certain since renouncing Calvinism; I have
at least been much happier." Ah, but is not happiness in
this life meaningless when compared with "truth?"

59.

The "Puritans" by repressing the enjoyment of life struck a blow
at folk culture generally—singing, dancing, plays, poetry, etc. By
doing this they opened the door for the arts to be more or less
antagonistic and antithetical to Christianity in the present age—
again the law of unintended (or opposite-intended) effects.

60.

The Germanic spirit still lives in all those who wander in
search of true feeling, who refuse to live only and exclusively
for profit. Sadly, this true desire is less commonly found
among the actual Germans themselves these days.

61.

Now, at the end of the Modern Age, with the failure of the Reformation, the Enlightenment and Science, it remains for us to redefine our understanding of mankind, our highest goals, and a vision of Truth. Only by pursuing these, apart from or transcendent of the failed Modernism, will there be anything but chaos and crude barbarism in the future.

62.

In a sense Hegel was right about the dialectic of history, but the teleology he had in mind is as doubtful as the logical nature of the syntheses. It is true though that one thing does seem to follow upon another in a temporal progression.

63.

How many have taken up the sabre or pistol, not out of hate, but simply of the demand to be taken seriously?

64.

For one's life to be farce at least one person must be taking it seriously; most often that person is oneself.

65.

Not only do the great men create the very taste by which they shall be appreciated, they create the terms by which the world and self shall be interpreted. For instance if one had never heard of the Will to Power, one would live simply and quietly without it.

66.

To make something *different* rather than *same*, is not to be equated with true creativity. A child can make something unique; only a genius can truly create.

67.

People scream so loudly for the sake of egalitarianism for everyone, in every circumstance, thus signifying their own deep doubt of self worth.

68.

If forced to choose, I would take love over the sex-act.
Thankfully these two are not, in fact, mutually exclusive—no
matter how much it may seem so in the present age.

69.

The same *Angst* and isolation which once drove higher men to
feats of greatness and creativity now lead the masses to neuroses
and violence. In fact, what one does with this inner turmoil is
the dividing line between the many and the higher men.

70.

The success of the higher men lies not merely in the strength of their
own will, ideas and virtue, but in the willingness of the masses to be
swept up in the majesty and glory of something higher than themselves.

71.

Of all the many varied experiences of human life,
being in love is the greatest of them all. By the same
token, loving is the greatest of the virtues.

72.

We are dependent on things so fragile for our very lives even,
yet because of the complexity of the system, we live without
conscious awareness of this fragility. It remains unclear
whether it is better to live in knowledge of the truth with the
accompanying angst, or to remain blissful in ignorance but with
the inevitable destruction due to the lack of fore-thought.

73.

The greater the mass of an object in motion, the longer it will remain
in motion due to its momentum. This principle also applies to the
grand system of contemporary society. No energy is currently being
added to keep it moving yet it continues to chug forward sluggishly
even though the foundations and spirit have been removed.

74.

Matter and material process are not the cause of idea and spirit, rather the opposite is true. This is the reason for the failure to solve most any problem in contemporary society: They attempt to change the matter while ignoring the spirit. Matter without spirit, it is literally "inanimate," a dead mass, *corpus mortuum.*

75.

If it is true that the artists are the prophets of society, then the future is indeed bleak, full of mad chaos and destruction.

76.

Tolerance and affirmation are not to be equated. We tolerate the sluggard but we do not affirm his laziness as a positive good. This is a key distinction to walk the line between totalitarianism on the one hand, and total cultural dissolution on the other.

77.

In the absence of legitimate trials and foes against which to strive, society will create straw-man enemies, in order to energize a phlegmatic populace (or control them). No society can long survive in the complete absence of a goal. The strength of any society is in direct proportion to how many and how strongly the folk strives against these foes—whether or not they be real or imagined.

78.

How is it that so much that is utterly clear remains hidden to the many? Have they not eyes to see, or do they simply refuse to do so?

79.

Perhaps the "puritans" refuse to drink because it forces them to remember their humanity.

80.

Dance is the human ritual where spirituality and sensuality meet. Thus any culture deficient in dance will be deficient in these two loci which are so necessary to maintain our humanity.

81.

The reason that nationalized industry does not work effectively
in the present age is that there is no longer a national pride
stronger than either selfishness or mere profit motive.

82.

The celebration (not toleration) of "multi-culturalism" is another
manifestation of the death-drive, but on a societal level. For how
will any human society or culture exist when even a common
tongue ceases to be? People who do not understand each other
do not live together in society. They live apart or wage war.

83.

Not the repression of sexuality, but when sexuality becomes allied to
Eros is the state of highest creativity, the greatest virtue, and beauty
achieved—for both society and individual. Contrariwise, sexuality,
when squandered, produces ugliness, weakness, and death.

84.

Music produces a visceral as well as spiritual response among all
who remain human. So the musician makes us feel his joy and
despair; this is his solace from feeling these things alone.

85.

How can civilization continue when, rather than sublimating the drives
that would destroy us, we encourage the same to become less and
less refined, resulting in a barbarism and animal instinct as the only
remaining impulses? The fact that we no longer even raise this question
shows that the primal nature has won; we no longer reflect, only react.

86.

History and Myth are both teleological and eschatological
in their own right. Both teach that there is a beginning,
a middle, and an end—like any good story. When rightly
understood, the whole of both is glorious and true.

87.

Psychotherapy arises necessarily in any culture after
the neglect of cleansing ritual and the confessional. Our
problems must necessarily find an outlet that includes human
understanding and reconciliation to self and other.

88.

Is specialization in vocation and languages yet another veiled apparition
of the Will to Power? After all, the specialist demands to be treated
as authoritative over and against all logic and common sense.

89.

Frustration is perhaps higher among the populace in democracy
than under a tyranny. For with tyranny one knows their voice
will not be heard. In democracy we are told that our voices will
be heard, that our voices have value. So when they go unheard
and unheeded the frustration mounts (hopefully) into a rebellion.
But woe for the inevitable result that awaits such a scenario!

90.

We are so very afraid of the results of human passions as
to have utterly anesthetized our humanity. Yet we wonder
why there is no adventure, no lofty goal, no love.

91.

Mixing of races is perhaps healthy and good on a biological
level, presuming both are fit for a given environment.
Mixing of cultures, without synthesis into a single and
integrated whole, will lead to certain destruction.

92.

Even *having* a book of aphorisms is pretentious.

93.

I disdain the bourgeois society of the 19th century as much as anyone,
but the alternatives suggested thus far have proven to be horrific.

94.
Late-night drunkenness is analogous to death, but being alive
the next morning, despite the pain is like resurrection.

95.
Only women can resent fate or destiny, though
both seem to shine on them the most.

96.
Shoot for Wagner, but settle for Brahms: a philosophy of life.

97.
The desire to make one's father proud led many a son to great
feats of courage, creativity or other virtue. Similar to this is the
desire to please God. So now imagine the stagnation and lowness
that would occur in culture when these desires are removed
and replaced with selfishness and disdain for one's father.

98.
" . . . in the narrow place of necessity . . ."

99.
The desire to create new life, to father children, biological or spiritual,
is somehow tied up in our longing for eternity. The fear and refusal to
follow this desire is another example of our longing only for death.

100.
Was the filthy, degrading and corrupt city of the industrial revolution
due merely to the poverty and high population density of the proletariat?
Or was it rather something deeper, the angst and resentment of a
people ripped apart from their rural place and from their entire folk
culture? People do not in general give up their entire way of life and
folk culture with felicity, but this was something the mind of the
industrialist and technocrat could not and cannot understand.

101.

The reason for the great burst of creativity in the natural and social sciences at the end of the 19th century and beginning of the 20th is that men like Weber, Jung, and Mach were not only analytically vigorous but they were steeped in the myth, literature and history of the whole epic of western culture. This gave them a sensitivity and spirit now lacking in today's scientists who are often merely technicians.

102.

It is equally preposterous when scientists expound on metaphysics as when philosophers pass judgment on theories of inorganic chemistry. Yet we are in such thralldom to *scientism* that we give weight to the opinion of the scientist on a subject in which he is no more an authority than a street performer.

103.

Many feel the angst and depression of a wasted life in the present age, and their sentiments are in fact more accurate than we would like to think. After all, only a very few perform a necessary function for societal survival or the more important aesthetic works that preserve the folk culture and national spirit. All the rest, quite literally, live a meaningless existence. But even worse is this: to feel neither angst nor depression in the midst of living that completely meaningless animal existence.

104.

There is a danger in *Dasein*, as we might be swept away by a dangerous mass-movement, or burnt up in a destructive passion. This danger, however, is worth the risk, for to live so analytically as to preclude *Dasein* is to be already dead.

105.

It is only by standing on the painful razor's edge between the abyss of black melancholy, darkest depression and the other extreme of mindless exuberance that true creativity can take place. This makes the life of the artist often tragic, often triumphant, but rarely anything in between. I would not have it any other way.

106.
The beauty of music is most profoundly tied to the sense of the tragic,
for the notes are as fleeting and unfastenable as the feelings they produce.

107.
We can never return to an earlier age or a previous level of
consciousness. To even attempt to do so would be folly. But to
ignore, repress or otherwise fail to synthesize with these previous
levels and times is also to preclude the possibility of transcending
our own age and our own self: The impasse of the present age.

108.
By normalizing homosexuality we do a great disservice to
those who once stood for sexual autonomy, rebellion and
counter-culture. Taking this away is to destroy the deep sensitivity
and artistic impulse once tied quite closely to such a lifestyle.
Tchaikovsky would have been a blasé composer in the present
age for his internal struggle would not have been so epic.

109.
The only thing more tragic than saying goodbye
is to leave and have nothing to say at all.

110.
We criticize and ridicule a person's taste if it seems underdeveloped,
wrong-headed or otherwise lacking. This implies that taste is, in some
sense, under volitional influence, that it can be directed and developed
to appreciate better things. Thus we are responsible even for taste.

111.
"For so long I've yearned for death, and I know not why."

112.
What if all of one's life were only and continually a series of grave
disappointments. Were our expectations of the gods too high?

113.

Men drink because it makes them feel like gods. This is why
sects and heresies of Christianity eschewed strong drink:
they feared divinity and the thought of feeling, let alone
becoming divine was too great and terrible to them.

114.

" . . . fear in a handful of dust . . ."—how is it such a short and simple
phrase can have such power to stir the soul in its very depths?

115.

The paper dolls tried so hard to please us and we scoffed in derision and
laughed them to scorn. Were we any better humans for our cynicism?

116.

We all exit the world in like manner as we entered—fearful,
naked and alone. There is universality in our midst, though
we often feel like we can share it with no one.

117.

The fatal flaw of the Will to Power is that it
destroys all those it overcomes.

118.

"I cannot promise to think on you in the moment of death, but be assured
that between now and then, I shall think on you many times my friend."

119.

Regret is a bitter poison that leads swiftly to death.

120.

"Why does the Devil have to be so warm, and humans
so cold, and God so distant?" (T.R.P.)

121.

Human life was not meant to be lived without drama. In the
absence of real conflict, we create it to fulfill this need. If we were
but mere animals, why should this be so? Rather why do we try
to explain away the lofty striving that at least some of us feel?

122.

"There was a time when I hated being myself so much, that
I learned an entirely different language in order to ease
into the charade of pretending to be someone else."

123.

Some avoid strong drink to avoid the accompanying reflection
and self-honesty that comes alongside a long draught; others
indulge to the point of stupor to avoid the same.

124.

If you always and immediately get what you desire, eventually
all desire will cease, and instead of nirvana, a personal hell will
result for one of the greatest pleasures of life will be gone: the
longing we experience in the absence of fulfilled desire.

125.

To be an American is to be, by definition, a sojourner; we have no true
Fatherland. We are all just a collection of variously motivated misfits.

126.

Nothing haunts quite so strongly or deeply as *Heimat*,
no matter where life's wanderings take one, and where
one resides for the remainder of the exile.

127.

Egalitarianism destroys most greatness while in incipient form. It, by
envy, spite and social training, precludes the rise of the higher men.

128.

Only the Englishman or perhaps his American counter-part
actually "concentrates" on drinking. Most others are caught
up in the rollicking joy of their compatriots in the beer hall.
This is yet another mistaking of the means for an end.

129.
One of the fatal flaws of fascism was that it had Will without
Love, while the modern leftists today feigns Love in the
absence of Will. For these deficiencies neither ideology could
be the source of transcending the current state of things.

130.
Life is not a contest to see who can have the most fun; neither is it one
to see who can have the least, wrapped up in a warped self-importance.

131.
Amerikanische Kultur ist jetzt überall—irony?

132.
God, love, suicide—only a few questions in life are truly worth our
reflection; if we fail to reflect on these, all else will be farce.

133.
Every day brings us one day closer to death—either
this is a glorious or most tragic of truths.

134.
Even now, alone before the mirror, you play
the part that's been given you.

135.
All this strength too, shall someday turn to dust.

136.
"I am tired of pouring my heart out, only to have
it spit back in my face at the end."

137.
In most cases Nietzsche was right: make yourself hard.

138.
"If I had never given myself away, I never would have had the
pain of rejection, but neither would I have been human."

139.
Dasein means the experience of exultation, but also the mortal pain of rejection. Even now, still among the living, I know it was worth it.

140.
The greatness and company of his ideas is how the intellectual provides himself solace from his solitude.

141.
Without beautiful literature, poetry, music, life would be very hard to bear at times. What then of those who seek petty diversion for their catharsis?

142.
There are generally two reasons one makes a study of a foreign language: to access on a deep level the great written works of a culture; to speak to beautiful women in their native tongue. Perhaps these are equally important.

143.
For some of the Calvinists, because they did not have "salvation by works" then work became their salvation.

144.
Each one must produce something of value for their given society; otherwise they have no right to remain a part of it.

145.
The Nation-State arose historically due to a conjunction of linguistic, racial and cultural solidarity. When "nations" no longer have these in common, nor are devoted to having them in common, how can they continue to exist?

146.
On the mountain top a man reflecting says to himself: "I fear that I think about myself and meditate upon my own ideas and aspirations too much." A voice from the vastness stretching out in front of him replies: "Every great man in the history of the world has done the same."

147.

All that we do in life is a more or less desperate attempt to counteract Time and Death. We exercise the body to slow its ageing and degeneration. We try to gain knowledge that will somehow give us the key to living forever. We pursue pleasures ruthlessly because it distracts us from the inevitable fate that awaits us all. The inherent goodness of Life, of Being moves us to grasp hold of it as long as we can. How then can they be finite?

148.

The Empire is nearing its end and the world is taking a deep breath before it plunges into a long dark night.

149.

Cassandra was perhaps the most cursed, the most tragic of all mortals because she could see the terrible fate that awaited her and her people, though they believed not her warnings. To have to await the evil and know it must arrive is the cruelest of tortures. Ignorance is what allows many to enjoy each of the moments leading up to the gathering storm. Now we ask whether is it better to have knowledge or to be ignorant. For my part, I do not fault the masses for their seemingly willful naivety yet I would not choose to relinquish my premonition of the fate that is coming upon us.

150.

Truth and knowledge, no matter how painful or tragic, are in fact always better than falsehood and ignorance. We ignore the truth at our own peril. There is often much tragedy tied to knowing the truth; this is what makes tragedy beautiful.

151.

When the passions of life are flowing, so too the font of the artist's pen.

152.

The malaise and ennui of the present-day West is in one part due to
our attainment of, and inability to transcend that long-sought goal:
democracy. When they threw down the barricades in Paris, many
were willing to die for the ideals of democracy, but having attained
the goal, it left us disillusioned because it did not bring the salvation
and utopia we yearned for, and still yearn for, in our souls.

153.

One theory is that the State was created in order to protect men
from each other, but now it exists more or less to perpetuate itself—
and the original functions, when present at all, are ancillary.

154.

Yearning for greatness is philosophical Idealism's
equivalent to the monk's search for eternal life.

155.

Writers were truly talented who crafted stories without the
simultaneous muse of music. That music is the highest muse is clear and
it is intuitive that the first authors should have written poetic songs.

156.

Start beating a drum and marching, and regardless of the cause,
many will join in and follow. For men, more than liberty, more than
justice, more than truth or any other higher thing, desire to join
themselves with others in a common cause, no matter what it be.

157.

"I do prefer the company of my fellow men, but had I never
been lonely and alone, I never would have written."

158.

To require humans to not be jealous, to extinguish all desire for
revenge, may in fact be good and useful, but it runs the danger of
also weakening the capacity to love passionately. It might remove
from us a very strong and integral part of our humanity.

159.

It is impossible to truly capture a moment, but the desire
and attempt to do so—this is why we write.

160.

Allusion in writing or speech is the Gnostic pleasure
of special knowledge, which one hopes will be shared
by the fellow initiate. Every allusion I make causes to
appear on my face that smirk of the archaic smile.

161.

Drinking alone is a dangerous proposition; I
recommend it only to the true poets.

162.

"Frisch weht der Wind
Der Heimat zu.
Mein irisch Kind
Wo weilest du?"

163.

English, French, German, Latin, Spanish, Russian, Ancient
Greek, Arabic, Hebrew—not necessarily in that order.

164.

"April is the cruelest month"—but what if one lives
in the southern hemisphere? Perhaps these lack the
sentiment to think of a month as cruel.

165.

Between the two, alcohol is a far more effective and trusty muse
than women. Now the *idea* of a woman—that surpasses all.

166.

Go on now, smile at your own cleverness, no one is looking.

167.

Food eaten in secret may indeed be sweeter, but
sometimes it is also less shameful.

168.

Music unleashes a passion stronger than any sin; this
is why moralists and pacifists fear music.

169.

How strange to indulge in folly, sin, or evil in an
attempt not to seem rude; this must be the most
forgivable and laughable type of moral offense.

170.

Why would I, why would anyone want to extinguish or
diminish the vigor of their human sensibilities? For this is
our very life! Yet our work, our entertainments, and our
addictions do this very thing—dead man walking.

171.

Though most disdain or fear it, certain Germans of the 19th century
will always be the ideal and the goal, at least if we are not to return all
the way to Greece. We still live in fear of the great and awful potential
of the fully impassioned human spirit applied to the whole of society.

172.

It is in fact virtue rather that vice to be willing, even desirous to die for
one's *patria*. If only we had a *patria* worth dying for! How fallacious then
our view in the present age, that treats such as criminals and madmen.

173.

Technology may not give us anything more important to
do, but it does give us something we believe to be quite
essential: a diversion from mortality, truth and meaning.

174.

Your life is made up of time. So if you are just "killing
time" then really you are just killing yourself.

175.

The intuition of our souls tells us that love is eternal.
Thus the bitterness and disillusion when what we thought
was love turns out to have been transitory.

176.

"Between the conception and the creation . . . life is very long."

177.

Regardless of how heroic the effort, one can never escape oneself,
even after death. This is either paradise or damnation.

178.

A well-earned cigar and a well-deserved long glass of Scotch
after a good night of writing—let the Baptists and Teetotalers be
scandalized! (Just wait till they read what was written as well!)

179.

Writing about writing, is there an end to the infinite regress?

180.

"Time heals all wounds." Some wounds, though, have cut us too
deep to be healed in the time contained in this life. In the next they
will either be healed once and for all, or burn us yet deeper.

181.

The fleeting things are often the most beautiful: a song, a sunset,
a dream. Yet somehow beauty is the most eternal thing.

182.

To begin to write, is to be somewhat arrogant, to think one has
something worthy of another's reading. By this same token all speech
is tainted by selfishness and arrogance (cf. Augustine's theory of
language). Must we really be so jaded in all that we think and do?

183.

Durkheim and the sociologists are in dialectic with the Existentialists
concerning individual and society. There is perhaps a very specific
reason why we have not yet transcended this dialectic.

184.

"Every Friday night, I fall in love on the dance floor, but the
next morning I struggle to even remember their names."

185.
The danger and responsibility of greatness is that one might
become a hideous monster. Though we hate to admit it,
if Hitler had been equal in his moral fortitude as he was in
his oratory, he very well might have saved the West.

186.
I long to become lost in a movement, a moment, a feeling: thus to lose
myself for a while. But the very fact that I am so aware of such a desire
means that I am likely too self-reflective to have such an experience.

187.
"If you knew you were going to regret it, then why did you do it?"
No answer has yet been found to this question.

188.
The danger of there being so many is that the best might get
lost in the morass of the multitude, were that even possible!

189.
How is being a scholar on a particular individual anything more than an
intellectualized cult of personality? Yet many scholars are simply this.

190.
Most great men must wait till after their death to be recognized
as such. If this is in fact the case, what is the point even?
Perhaps it were better to be an unknown without angst or
travail but joy till the end of one's days. If there is no higher or
transcendent ideal this latter is then the better of the two.

191.
For the first time in history a non-musician individual can
enjoy music in complete solitude. Due to our complex circuitry
we no longer require the presence of the musicians.

192.

Our moments of great sorrow, or great joy—these we long to share with another person. Perhaps this is the reason we pray at such times in the absence of other humans. That we no longer experience either great sorrow or joy also would then explain why we no longer pray.

193.

Why should it be that beauty, tragedy, and joy all should bring us to the same response: tears.

194.

It is far easier to bear being misunderstood than to be understood and rejected. This is one reason why the sensitive artist veils himself in his works so that only those who truly are interested, who love him, will bother to seek and find what lies behind the veil.

195.

At times, Fate herself seems quite spiteful.

196.

For some it was a natural-feeling temptation contrary to nature. To the more sensitive, it was the quickest way to receive a plethora of physical and emotional affirmation.

197.

Ego vici mundum.

198.

Where the pace of life is slow: good for leisure, poor for battle.

199.

That many of us in the present age must *search* for something to do most of the time is a testimony to our advance in technology. That the vast majority fritter away the hours in mindless diversion is a testimony to our decadence.

200.

We had great hunger, but after eating our fill we were left strangely unsatisfied.

201.

Few things produce more angst than being a foreigner, a stranger in a strange land. This angst explains the distrust that can lead to rage. It also explains the often criminal and subversive nature of unwelcome foreigners who in their homeland would have been perhaps upright and law abiding citizens.

202.

Are most crimes committed due to a misunderstanding of language; is evil merely a confusion? Or is there some malice that resides deeper in our souls, something that would break out and do evil even with the utmost clarity of words?

203.

Memory colors all history, personal or otherwise. Our remembrance of an incident makes it either felicitous or atrocious, more so than the reality of the thing. Once in the past, what more remains of a moment than memory? So in a sense memory, not history, is all that exists of the past.

204.

History is the study and critique of metanarratives from the past, from the perspective of the ruling metanarrative of the present time. Interpretation makes the event either a great triumph or a great evil, or simply unimportant, depending on one's metanarrative.

205.

All we are relatively sure has existence are souls, or minds if you prefer. Every day I take a leap of faith that material is also real. It seems to work.

206.

To be better off dead would seem a truly sad estate. But that the most miserable cling to the last scrap of life to the bitter end is another testimony to the goodness of Being. On the other hand though the saints are truly better off dead, often they are the ones who have the most reason to remain in this world—yet they freely give it up.

207.
In writing aphorisms I hope to be compared with Nietzsche,
Epectitus and Pascal, but I fear that I will be compared
with Franklin and the platitudes of aged women.

208.
After the advent of rigorous historical investigation it was only those
who died young who could grow to mythic fame because the brevity of
their life prevented disillusion with their short-comings and allowed
us to ponder our favorite question of all—what might have been?

209.
When compared to the higher men of Europe or Antiquity,
the American heroes seem too much like comic book
characters or paper cut-outs. They indeed have little depth,
but perhaps there is a certain virtue to simplicity.

210.
People who are full do not glut themselves at banquets. Those
who do glut themselves remain disturbingly unfulfilled.

211.
We return to places that are familiar to us, because familiarity breeds
fondness. When everything has changed upon our return we feel
cheated and robbed of our sentiments that were associated with that
place. So in a land where everything always changes there will be little
depth of emotion connecting the inhabitants to where they live. It seems
unlikely to be able to love anything, if one cannot love his home.

212.
The Celtic music, with its droning bagpipe has such a force and
melancholy as to inspire men, otherwise woefully out-manned,
to march bravely to their death: This is beauty at its best.

213.
How is it that one can imagine a world more beautiful and more perfect
than this one? If the imagined world is better, how can it be less real?

214.
"I truly believe that I could save America, possibly the whole world. Delusions of grandeur, megalomania and mathematical possibility aside for a moment, am I morally vicious for not even making the attempt?"

215.
Is it prideful or profound if one's own poetry brings one to tears?

216.
Qui dormiunt, evigilabunt

217.
La vida es sueño.

218.
Once upon a time, music was a deep, moving, and a profound part of culture, able to inspire the heart toward great humanity. Now most music has become simply the diversion of the masses, allowing them to ignore life and its true drama, providing a pseudo-narrative escape to allow them to flee from truly living.

219.
Culture and its arts are often much like wine; none who have tried the old care to drink the new. And as it has been said ever and anon, new wine cannot be put into old wineskins or it will burst them asunder.

220.
One's *Heimat* is the place of childhood, the familiar landscapes, smells and seasons. Most importantly it is where one's fathers are buried.

221.
In the present age we claim that our quality of life is greatly improved from the past, but when we say this it is almost entirely in reference to an abundance of material possessions. Is not life more than food and drink, more than clothing and a mass of useless and paltry things? Strange how we fail to remember or emulate the wise men from the ancient past who strove for and taught about a life more abundant than the abundance of goods.

222.

We disdain kings, lords and tyrants, along with the very rich
and scoff. Yet we all seem bent on emulating their luxury
in our own lives. Do we then disdain ourselves?

223.

Knowledge is power. All the more reason men ought to
learn virtue as prerequisite to anything else, because once
given the power of knowledge without virtue, they will
almost certainly use it to wield against the Good.

224.

Every piece of knowledge is a window upon the whole. T.S. Eliot
can teach us much about everything, even in a single poem

225.

It is the latent Protestant spirit in me that causes a feeling of guilt
for all the moments spent doing something not strictly "useful."

226.

The joy of hearing music is to be lost in the *Dasein*.

227.

Heidegger wrote of *Dasein* in an age when falsity, propaganda, repression
and mass entertainment were coming into there own. Is it any wonder?

228.

Why should it be that the greatest moments of
joy and of sorrow be experienced alone?

229.

"I am running out of new ideas." But there are no "new ideas." Ideas
exist independently of our thinking them. We do not come up with new
ideas, only apprehend the already existent and eternal form. This is why
there is such a unity of thought and a true similarity of philosophy across
ages and cultures. Though, the skeptics still argue about *Kleinigkeiten.*

230.
To feel deeply and truly is not a birth-right. Like all sensibilities
is can be practiced and cultivated. There is then a moral hierarchy
even with emotions. It is clear that to feel sorrow along with
those who morn is morally better than to feel glee at another's
misfortune. This is obvious but many claim non-culpability with
the phrase: 'I cannot change how I feel.' This statement does
not exonerate the joyful murderer, for it simply is not true.

231.
Those without a metaphysical religion and thus some hope for
continuation of personal existence after death generally take one
of two paths: they run after life with great gusto, trying to squeeze
out every drop of fleeting pleasure before the curtain falls; the other
type lives the life of quiet and stoic resignation and desperation, too
depressed by the inevitable and final end to even attempt to enjoy
the few days given. Both these paths are vanity, a dry wind blowing
through dusty deserted streets. That neither of these paths lead to
flourishing should be evidence enough that they are not true.

232.
Even facing death was not enough to inspire me to truly live. Only
the loss of love, the much greater death, could convince me to live the
truly joyful and contented life. It is really not so strange that great loss
is the door to great gain that the path of life passes through death.

233.
Any act of Will is both triumphant and tragic. It is triumphant
because Will is a reflection of the part of us that is god-like, free
to choose, and powerful to change; it is tragic because each act of
Will limits us, narrows the possibilities for the future, and narrows
the world itself. To choose one thing is to reject many others.
There is a small death that occurs because of this. For that reason, a
strong act of Will often brings with it a deep sense of melancholy.
Yet this is the dialectic within which we are called to live.

234.
A beautiful edifice, a beautiful painting, a beautiful woman—how sad
to know that I shall see none of these ones again after the travel's end!

235.
System, no matter how genius, will always fail in the absence of Spirit.

236.
Some men write history to claim participation with the great actors of history. Other men write history to explain and justify their current hegemony in the world. Still others write history to condemn or indemnify the past occurrences responsible for their current plight.

237.
When paper and ink were quite expensive, how did that affect the content, not to mention the amount of what was written?

238.
"I am a stranger in a strange land . . . but then I always was."

239.
There is a certain moral satisfaction that goes along with seeing the sunrise.

240.
It was not the German race that was superior, but rather the German spirit. Once this confusion between flesh and spirit occurred (for spirit must always supersede flesh), then that great spirit also began to wane.

241.
Only those who work hard or drink hard enjoy the rest of a very deep sleep. Strange how these opposites should reap the same reward.

242.
Why should we scoff at the writer who is purposefully archaic, obscure or even anachronistic? Is there something about the writing of our age that is so obviously better?

243.

Great cultures are the ones we know about. The specialist has little right to pass judgment on this. Cultures live and thrive (even after their death) due to some sort of preservation and evangelization. If no one is excited enough about a given culture to spread its dogmas far and wide, then that culture will necessarily die.

244.

Creativity in the early morning is a rare occurrence, as all the wild spirits seem to be asleep. The morning, however, is sometimes just very, very late at night.

245.

In the city of man are not our goals ostensibly the same? Peace, justice, prosperity, beauty? Yet we stand in enmity against one another, even within our own society.

246.

As soon as I was able to talk I began a lifelong love affair with words.

247.

"By the cool serenity of his face, none could have guessed the stormy passions that raged in his heart."

248.

"Look 'round the habitable world, how few Know their own good, or knowing it pursue."

249.

Somewhere along the line between the 1950's and now, the American dream has become a nightmare.

250.

Instinct is the scientific word for the Fall of Man. Instinct tells us to preserve self at all cost, to breed with impunity, to dominate, to oppress, to run away when convenient, to be greedy, and all other manner of vice. In the Fall we lost a great measure of our humanity. So, only by overcoming instinct do we rise above the animals and again become human. That we have a choice to do so is what makes us unlike the animals: morally culpable when we blindly follow instinct.

251.

Science, with its proofs, analyses and dogmas is as much a meta-narrative as it is anything, created to explain, according to a coherent system, the phenomena of life. It thus creates structure and intelligibility in the world, but may not have given us anything better to go on for the really important things than religion did.

252.

Without words, the world as we know it would cease to exist.

253.

The value of an aphorism is that it shoots strait to the heart of the matter and does not allow the reader to lose himself in the minutiae; he is confronted without escape.

254.

It seems that I listen to far less music when compared with the many today, who constantly have their ear-wires pumping sounds into their brains. Because of this I believe that I enjoy music more when I do in fact listen to it. Yet sometimes I wonder whether there is not something deeper still: an aversion to listen because I fear the power of music, and what the muse might inspire me to do, even against my will. Perhaps it was for this reason that many of the moralists and fundamentalists have preached against music; they likewise feared its power, and our powers to resist it.

255.
One might easily argue that when compared with the
Germanic cultures of 19th century Europe, that none other
had a culture whatsoever. Were this the case is still no
justification for liquidating other races and cultures.

256.
Imagine the immense power of the Germanic races had they
united for good instead of in-fighting and essentially destroying
one another. Alas, strife, jealousy and conflict among brothers has
been the rule since Cain and Abel, Romulus and Remus, et al.
It is now, sadly, part of our nature to fight those closest to
us, those with whom we should be the most united.

257.
Had the poets not given us the words, how
should we have ever been able to feel?

258.
In a sense Hitler did to Nietzsche, what Marx did to Hegel (all were
Germans, mind you). He took a philosophy that had strong roots in
Idealism (though not always Kantian), but applied it to race instead
of economics (as Marx did). We now see the results of reducing
Ideals to the merely physical aspect. So it is with all reductionists.

259.
Who will be the philosopher to bring Nietzsche and Pascal
together, in a synthesis that will go beyond the two?

260.
History must not stagnate, either by holding on too strongly
to the past, nor in utter iconoclasm concerning the past.

261.
This brave new world is swiftly coming to its end, and I fear
for those who are not prepared for those days of woe.

262.
Without being at least slightly enamored with one's own ideas, there
would be no reason to write them down. A certain amount of healthy
pride is pre-requisite to sharing good things with the world.

263.
This once-strong Folk has now become weak, selfish and decadent.
The land of barn-stormers and home-run hitters has become
the slough of lazy observers who watch and imagine life without
bothering to live it. Who knows if they will be roused even
when the barbarians bring the fight to their very gates . . .

264.
The truest of true critiques cuts to the heart of both
our own times and to every other time as well.

265.
At the bottom of the bottle of wine, all men are faced with
these: mortality and eternity. Those who continue to drink
for the sake of oblivion do so at their own peril.

266.
If my opinions are so offensive, why do I continue to make
them known? If it were not for some higher good this
would either be a masochism or simply misanthropy.

267.
The world is not yet ready for these ideas, yet when it finally is,
the same ideas will no longer be interesting, only a commonplace
and a given. So it is, so it was with the thinkers who gave the
whole world a perspective after their time. This is why Cicero
seems so very bland—his ideas have more or less permeated
Western thought completely. What is revolutionary today will
become the very "linguistic construction of reality" tomorrow.

268.
These words too shall turn into dust. Yet the bother
to write them, another futile grasp at eternity?

269.

Why do we disagree with such vehemence and passion, when both of our opinions shall be neither heard nor implemented?

270.

Perhaps there is something even more important and powerful than people: ideas . . .

271.

If we are not allowed to be proud of our shining moment, then what is the point of any striving for excellence whatsoever?

272.

What shape will politics, education, and economics take when there is no longer enough physical energy left for mass movements or universal systems? We will not even know what is going on across the world; neither will we have the energy to care.

273.

To the artist, the pole of madness is to be preferred to the other extreme of depression. For on the brink of madness there is much energy, much creativity, much activity of all kind. In the slough of depression though, there is only idleness, ennui, listlessness—to the artist this is the same as death. Yet all the same, many an artist has idled away his best years of creativity in the grip of an insurmountable melancholy.

274.

To be overly slavish to the past in one's sentiments is to be overly obsessed with tragedy because remembrance nearly always idealizes. Thus, this makes out of the glory of our history an insurmountable standard for the future. On the contrary this mythic "golden age" whether true or not, and toward which we might aspire is in fact a way to try and overcome the same tragic over-idealization. To have no ideals at all, past or future, this is to refuse to engage the dialectic.

275.

While the known world was put to torch and sword by the barbarians, a few quiet monks prayed, read and wrote. They saved nearly all worth saving from the past, and not by force of arms, but by a firm will dedicated to the True, the Good, and the Beautiful—these shall never be vanquished as long as men be men.

276.

What else ought a man do than enjoy the moment, put his hand to useful work, do good and hope in eternity? What joy would be in the world were all to turn from vanity to these few simple things!

277.

Ideas and philosophy shall continue to hold importance after the system crumbles, because these stand above the details of the machine and have a universal application. History too will have importance, but the way we view the occurrences of the past will be radically different than now. In fact many of the high points of "modern" history will be looked upon as black moments that led us to the coming destruction.

278.

Having been etherized for so long, shall we be able to face reality when it comes rushing back upon us with a vengeance?

279.

There is no travail except that which is common to man; the difference between felicity and misery is the manner in which we deal with the same.

280.

The company of humans who can meet one in mind and spirit is truly the most satisfying of all delights, but the second is to be alone and ponder, read or write and to meet in spirit the realm of Ideas.

281.

Escape is the mentality of all Americans, for they are only Americans due to their desire to escape another place, whether that be Europe or Asia. Escape, though, does not put its hand to the inevitable and difficult work of building a greater society. That is why the divisions are so great in what they call the United States (perhaps still thus called by the time this is in print); those who do not want to compromise, only escape to a utopia of their own making; this an impossible task.

282.

The content of creative work cannot be willed into existence, but the initiating of creativity in oneself often requires that act of will to set it into motion. Will is the catalyst by which the Muse often moves.

283.

In this present age of too many decisions and overload of activity, it is not surprising that many should turn to the philosophy of Buddhism. For by extinguishing will and desire, one is able to absent themselves from the bombardment of questions, decisions, false answers, and chaos of the present age. Nirvana may or may not be waiting for those who make this attempt.

284.

Imagine the immense power of thought, memory, and creativity the philosophers and poets must have had before there existed little scraps of paper upon which to scribble every little idea as it came (this written by hand in a small, black, leather-bound notebook).

285.

Anonymity is not something we ought to desire;
it is a sign of hidden, anti-social drives.

286.

All men yearn to take part in something greater than themselves. This is not to be ignored, and is more than enough explanation for family, society, mass movements, religion and even philosophy. As this is part of our nature, it is something to be directed and cultivated, not suppressed or denied.

287.
Playing the fool is certainly better than actually being
one; it is at least self-conscious and self-consciousness
is the first step toward escaping folly.

288.
Napoleon at St. Helena: to have been the ruler of the world and
to have whiled away the rest of one's days at complicated games
of solitaire. How tragic it is to lose one's status as a god! What
is more tragic: the quietly contented Englishmen who defeated
him and never had a pure desire for greatness themselves, only
a policy that made sure their ledger lines were all in order.

289.
To those whose quest is clear—they are blessed by
having a life always filled with purpose.

290.
The part of us that lasts forever, this we ignore and fear most of all.
Yet all men live as if that temporal part of us is something eternal.

291.
We have all breathed far too much of the same air as
Foucault and must be purged and do penance.

292.
Education is now primarily about molding the good citizen,
not cultivating genius (perhaps it always was?). Though there is
nothing terribly wrong with the citizens being good, the "good
citizen" and great genius have rarely been the same man.

293.
The reluctance to share one's deepest passions and treasured
ideas and sentiments stems from the fear that these will be
spurned by the other, and the pain that results from having
something we love so deeply being denigrated. Yet all that
we love, and is truly good, can and must be shared.

294.
I have been accused of writing tautologies and though this is certainly better than writing falsities, still I do confess that I write them.

295.
Whether the world as we know it is coming to an end or not, the lifestyle of most of the non-western and non-urbanized world will not be changed substantially. To most, geographically if not numerically, the future, whether it bring good or evil, matters less than one in New York City might think.

296.
Before all work can become dignified, the consumer must first develop a taste for and then a demand for works made with dignity. As long as people are content to consume garbage they will never be served truly good delicacies and consequently dignified work will not exist in any great amount.

297.
Plato warned us against accepting "truth" for merely aesthetic reasons. Then he went on to found his "Republic" on a purely contrived allegory. Thus, neither pure reason, nor pure feeling may be the ultimate arbiter of truth.

298.
Music is the muse of the soul; it inspires greatness, sacrifice and directed love. So it should be no surprise that the greatest European composers of the 19th century helped inspire the desire for political greatness among the Germanic peoples of the 20th.

299.
To understand minds and feel the passion of soul, of men as far removed from myself and each other in place and time as Sophocles and Marlowe . . . this is the immense universality and power of spirit.

300.
By desiring ease of life and only comfort men seal their own destruction, for from this perverse desire, contrary to the nature of human-ness, shall come no thing into their existence that truly could be called life.

301.

The truly creative are always highly sexual as well, that part of Eros living strongly within them and desiring to come out, only that this sexual urge has transcended the merely physical and brought them into a realm beyond the animal into the spiritual and transcendent.

302.

Throughout there has been a tension, a dialectic between justice and beauty. It is only when these two meet with a kiss that human society can fully flourish.

303.

Decadence is merely the most pleasurable and thus in a way the most pathetic and tragic manifestation of a society's collective *Thanatos* syndrome.

304.

Did pederasty (modern-style homosexuality did not as exist as far as we know) develop in certain Greek city-states as the "natural" consequence of lack of birth control, over-population, urban living, the exclusion of women from public life, all this combined with either inability or unwillingness to overcome or sublimate the male sex drive? After all, this vice was all but unknown amongst their rural counterparts in Macedon and Thessalia.

305.

Often the drives most intense yet opposed are found within the same man. For instance the *Thanatos* drive and the drive to procreate. The synthesis of these two is intercourse which is to be likened unto dying and yet the seed of new creation is the natural result.

306.

Sexuality without passion leads only to impotence and death.

307.

First there were the gods, then the heroes, then saints, and now the mass man who knows none of them.

308.
A city built in a day shall burn in a minute, and every
house without foundation is easily cast into the sea.

309.
If I knew every fact, every language, every feeling, everything in the
whole world, would that not be some assured way of saving my immortal
soul as well? This in fact was the error of Faust—human, all too human.

310.
The Archaic smile: the hero's internal knowledge that the
way to cheat death is to rule over it and make it one's servant,
using death as a means to win glory and immortality.

311.
By their scars we know of their yearning for death, for immortality.

312.
"We are Americans; we are all exiles."

313.
If an African nation were to expel the European races from her
midst, we would call its people patriots, freedom fighters, and
heroes. Yet if a European nation were to expel its non-national
minorities we would call them fascists, Nazis and bigots.
Contemporary morality then, is not based on reason, or even logical
consistency. It is based on sentiment created almost arbitrarily by
those who are loudest and most convincing in their rhetoric.

314.
Suae quisque faber est fortunae.

315.
I have put the whole of my passion and heart into these ideas and
ideals, the highest for which I would gladly die. At the same time
the world yawns and goes slumping along toward its destruction,
disturbingly apathetic even to the most radical and disturbing
of these ideas as something too *drôle* to do anything about.

316.
"I am just a man"—were words more tragic ever spoken?

317.
Ultimately the mass man with his small morality
destroys the beauty of humanity, for only the hero can
be truly tragic, and thus beautiful in his time.

318.
Why should it have been that the one tin soldier who was unique
and therefore special and superior in a way, was only thus by virtue
of his defect in lacking a leg? Should he not have been all that the
rest were and even more? Why should weakness be glorified over
strength, ugliness over beauty? This is not to say that weakness
or ugliness are to be reviled, but neither should they be lauded
for their own sake as if by their very *nature* they were good.

319.
"Modern" Art: Once our senses have been jarred
by ugliness *ad nauseam*, what then?

320.
We do not know whether this "work of art" is "good" until
we hear the artist's famous and popular name. Otherwise it is
merely the work of a somewhat talented but neurotic child.

321.
Folk Art: it does in fact help keep the mass of men in their culture,
which is a laudable goal. It does best when it is decorative and useful
while being integrated with the rest of the folk culture, but why
would we want to try and immortalize anything so un-heroic?

322.
They all gained independence from Spain nearly two centuries ago; they
are overly proud of this fact. In the intervening years there is little to
show for this "freedom." One wonders then whether it would have been
better to have remained part of something grander and more glorious,
certainly more humane, than being an economic satellite of the British.

323.

If one does not use freedom to do either good or great things, then
it were better to be a servant under a master pursuing such ends.
Freedom, ill-used, and ill-defined is not a categorical good.

324.

Degeneration is the natural tendency of all things if left to
themselves, matter, flesh, institutions, and societies. It requires
will and striving to countermand ruin and destruction.

324.

The meek shall inherit the earth, for the strong
shall slay each other in mortal combat.

325.

Sex, switchblades and cocaine is perhaps not
enough upon which to base a culture.

326.

Since all the gods, demi-gods, and heroes have died or faded
into oblivion, how do we then justify our own lives?

327.

However beautiful it may seem, I do not desire to
be lulled to death by sweet melancholy.

328.

Art should not exist to give us a more acute and intense window upon
our prosaic and mundane lives, sad or happy though they be. It exists to
show us the ideal, the heroic, the transcendent. By combining passion
with form it ought to elevate our spirits and take us beyond ourselves
into realms of beauty and glory of which we now can barely dream.

329.

Aristotle told us that if we categorically doubt our teachers, then we
can never know anything. This is quite true and thus all the more
important that our teachers love virtue, which is the better part of truth.

330.
Theory of Criminality: violence against a society due
to resentment regarding the failed promise of equality.
Since men are not equal by nature, to promise them this
was either naïve or insidious. There is a fatal flaw in the
incipient ideology of the Enlightenment democracy.

331.
Justice: law comes from an integrated people using their knowledge
of nature to arrive at conclusions concerning law and justice. I
would certainly hope that no one would fault a man for killing
the one who brutally raped his child; he is meting out natural
justice on the heinous offender. Yet in our current society the
just avenger would still be punished. Why? If none would fault
him for such just revenge why should the "system" punish him?
This is another example of the system supplanting the people.

332.
"Knowledge too is certain death."

333.
After the post-structuralists have broken down every icon,
every hero, every law, every virtue, every truth, then all
that remains is categorical suspicion of motives, distrust and
sterile analysis. When there is no history, culture, literature
or philosophy worthy of our respect, what then?

334.
When it comes to the flourishing of beauty in a
culture, almost as important as the creator, the genius
himself, is an audience of sensitive and cultivated
participants who love and appreciate the best.

335.
"Why are they so utterly beautiful when angry or in tears?"

336.
Love only comes through suffering.

337.
If ever you desire something unto death, it
were better you not have it just yet.

338.
"Well I want to die"—the ultimate moment of human
life is no longer tragic, but rather farce.

339.
Since the world is now thought of primarily in terms of
commodities, supply and demand, why should not human
life itself be held cheaply when in such abundance?

340.
The teacher is not the one who primarily transfers
knowledge; a book can do that well enough. Rather, he
is a human who can inspire that which is of greatest
moment. The true teacher then *must* inspire love for what
is good in his students. Therefore all things not worthy
of being loved neither are worthy of being taught.

341.
Only the second born strive to be greatest in the
world; the first simply inherits his greatness.

342.
There is no surer sign of the death of a culture than that
the people, rather than participate actively in their society,
passively receive diversions and mindless entertainments.

343.

Protestantism began, in some respects, with an emphasis of knowledge over feeling, even to the neglect of the emotive part of humanity almost entirely (no art, little or no music, churches stripped of icons). This extreme brought on the swing toward pietism centuries later and eventually the emotionalist reaction of the Great Awakening. Those souls, starved for beauty, yearned for expression but outside the boundaries of tradition and thus quickly into absurdity and grotesque emotionalism. Thus once set free from the stern traditions of their iconoclasts forbearers their spiritual "awakening" resembled the Bacchic more than anything Christian. Being unshackled from the moorings of the church, this ignorant and ill-formed people had nothing left to protect them from themselves and their own excesses, leading to a ridiculous expression that reasonable men soon eschewed and thus the decline of Protestantism among most except the simplest and unrefined of thought.

344.

Both the gods of the Greeks and the God of the Hebrews are anthropomorphic (it would not make sense for God to be any other way?). The difference was that while in later myth Zeus represented the permissive immorality of a decadent society, and often the worst of human vices (despite shining moments of virtue and greatness), the Hebrew God, on the other hand, metes out justice, is a fiery and vengeful storm god, who also is merciful and represents the best of human passions. It is impossible that the highest being would not also be the most beautiful, the most virtuous, and the best. We fear what this might mean for us who are called to be gods in our little corner of the cosmos.

345.

If all work is a vocation and therefore equally religious in nature, then there is no special virtue in the strictly spiritual life. It should be no surprise that secularization eventually results from this doctrine.

346.

Drinking often begins as a social activity, but given enough time and effort, no matter how many are present, each one ends up drinking with only himself.

347.

We have now entered the building; it could be a hospital, a business, a
government office. Little placards point us the way to the bookstore,
the gymnasium, the coffee shop and the restrooms. Oh, this is in fact
supposed to be a "church." But the space feels far from sacred and nothing
mysterious or awesome resides here; it feels more like a Hollywood
studio, complete with façades and lighting effects. Is it any wonder . . .

348.

"The medium is the message." How can we even attempt to
convey deep and solemn truth through media that are inherently
silly and ephemeral? Our truth then quickly becomes farce.

349.

Is salvation a moment or a process? Do we really have no
need to strive alongside what has been graciously given? Can
flesh be transformed in an instant and without pain?

350.

These so-called disciples of Christ, walking the streets in search
of converts, judging by their uniforms, look suspiciously like
the students of capitalism and the protégés of accountants.

351.

Though perhaps an *ad hominem* fallacy, it still seems unlikely to receive
a true message, if the messenger be too ridiculous to be taken seriously.

352.

Jesus Christ was not a capitalist; he was not a scientist; he
was neither republican nor Marxist. He cannot be named
or numbered amongst such paltry categories.

353.

Here are the Holy Scriptures—but even these when
mass printed, when so easily and freely had, how could
they not be demeaned in value and held cheaply?

354.

I wanted to find the Christ, so I went to the place that
some called his house. I spoke with those who called
him their friend; I waited. He did not appear nor return,
so I went to find him in another place, and if not there,
I will continue to search till I have found him.

355.

God, like Shakespeare has the delightful habit of using the Fool to
tell us a profound truth, though the Fool himself not realize it.

356.

These new demagogues are so drunk with their power over
the mindless herd of the masses that even during their speeches
they cannot help but sway and quiver with inebriation. Yet
what great feat is it to cut to pieces a paper tiger?

357.

All these words are no substitute for a single moment
of bold action. When speech does not reflect, refine
or inspire real action then it is like the blowing of a
wind hither and thither, without source or goal.

358.

My soul and mind pine for strong, even violent action
and the impotence of inaction leads to a malaise
and apathy; these quickly lead to death.

359.

Just because God calls the weak, the lowly, the poor, and the
feeble, does he not also want the strong, the beautiful, the wise
and the powerful? Nor does God speak untruth and call ugliness
beauty, nor does he call weakness strength. He merely clarifies
that the lowly are called just as much as the higher, and puts in
order the types of beauty and power in their proper hierarchy.

360.

All groups allow entrance either by birth or conversion. Birth-right based groups tend to be exclusive of outsiders who do not share ethnic and cultural roots with them. Conversion-based groups (which tend to be either philosophical or religious) can be multi-ethnic but to maintain their solidarity necessitates an intensity of conversion experience and an oath one swears to the doctrines necessary for cohesion.

361.

The liberal theology of no sin, no cross, no divine Christ, no Passion, no drama, no plaint in the night, no redemption, no glorious resurrection is wrong on many accounts (historically and otherwise), but most acutely in this: their metanarrative is boring, lacks spirit, diminishes beauty and divinity to the ugly and the pedestrian. I have no patience for those who reject triumph and despair, who want to reduce man to anything less than god-like status by reducing the stormy *Yahweh* to some bland, banal and silly old man. Why would they want such a paltry and boring story; why would they cast aside the truest myth?

362.

Once the masters of the houses of usury were too ashamed to show their faces in the house of God; now the banker swaggers in and takes his seat in the front without the least bit of shame.

363.

There is more than mere cognitive content to all communication. Often the non-cognitive is more important. Until this is recognized as true, much ugliness will be justified as the form remains ignored in favor of content. Can we not have both?

364.

If we Christians have been crucified to the world, why do we seem to be so enthralled with it still?—the nice house in the suburbs, the usury based portfolio, the rape of the earth, the economic oppression of the third world, and the fat comfort of our sloth, how is it we do not see the depth of our hypocrisy? The cross is a glorious hope, but also a high calling to die to all these transitory things.

365.
Some say that we have reached the limit of language in its ability to accurately describe or discuss anything. Why then are those who remain dogmatic about words? Simply this—to control thought and feeling—in a word: Power. This is the worst kind of tyranny of all though, for those manipulating the language are purely mercenary in their use of it, and do not even believe what they say. However, there may be some salvation left for us that transcends language, for God shows us himself in symbol and action, not words alone.

366.
"All happiness is a forgetting, in drink, in dance, in song; all remembrance is pain, deep and lasting, but pain brings truth, and only truth can set us free."

367.
It's all a game, but there is no satisfaction, no enjoyment, in fact nothing at all, unless one treats this game with utter seriousness, all the while maintaining on one's face the grin of the archaic smile.

368.
One of the strongest arguments against evolution, sexual selection, and survival of the fittest is this: the ancients seemed so beautiful, glorious, and god-like. Now, humanity the progeny of long generations, that should be moving ever higher, seems to be a confederacy of dunces.

369.
No one respects a fat face; such is the breeding ground for revolt.

370.

Without being able to stop, to be still, and to savor a moment, true
satisfaction eventually becomes impossible because stillness is an
inherently reflective state of mind. Thus if we are always distracted
from the moment, all enjoyment is lost. Cultivated distraction
ends up in destroying the capacity to enjoy anything whatsoever.
Therefore it is no surprise that in this age of distractions, there is little
satisfaction. The most insidious though is that there are many who
have lined their pockets, who have a strong vested interest in keeping
us discontent and distracted—always chasing the next thing. They
are the modern devils who laugh and sneer while humanity becomes
a heap of frazzled neurotics, without joy, without purpose, without
goal and often without even knowing how much is being lost.

371.

Between Historicism and Modernism lies a real expression of
the human spirit, capable of genuine creativity, integration and
purpose. It is possible, yea likely, that anything we have ever done
worthy of our humanity was neither in slavery to profit motives,
nor to history, nor to vice or any other thing. True freedom bursts
forth in beauty and all ugliness is slavery to some sub-human
thing. Our humanity now seems enslaved to illegitimate ends and
this is why few spirits can be roused to genuine excitement in
the participation of human society. We are vaguely aware of our
slavery without knowing exactly where it comes from; we only feel
it deep in our hearts in the quiet, lonely moments of the night.

372.

Nothing is harder to accept than that all of one's life, one's goals, one's
time has been utterly wasted and pissed away. This is why Croesus of
Lydia was so vexed with Solon regarding the story of Tellus, whom
Solon estimated the most blessed among mortals, and not Croesus
himself, who had spent much time accruing wealth. This is also why
the establishment cannot change itself; this would be to admit it has
all been a waste. How could anyone admit the unimportance of those
things that took a lifetime to gain? So it is with the Americans. They sold
their souls for material goods, the pseudo mansions, petrol monsters
that enslave them, and all other expensive toys they desire and attain.
To admit it was not worth it after all is to admit their own damnation.

373.
The true test of joy is whether one can be alone of
an evening and it be the best of one's life.

374.
Another problem with modern media is that they are
inescapable and oppressive. It is not only that what they convey
is essentially unimportant and/or false. We are so tightly
bound in their iron cage that we are all being coerced into
hearing their message and participating in their banality.

375.
Three proofs of the goodness of the monastic movement in Europe:
the preservation of the best of classical culture through devotion
of their lives to the copying of manuscripts; the development of
Gregorian chant from Greek and Hebrew musical sources and
the later polyphonies that arose from it; finally, the perfection
of the art of brewing beer. Without these three it would be hard
to claim that civilization had survived the fall of Rome. Yet the
former two stand neglected in our age, and beer brewing has only
recently been renewed, and that most often by non-monks.

376.
Alexander the Great, St. Francis, Keats, Schopenhauer, Tolstoy:
can I be the reincarnation of all of these? Or at least let their
spirit live again in me? It is not enough to observe and to know
to truly gain humanity; one must feel and one must act!

377.
Idealist and Existentialist: the idealist says that a man, an idea, a
culture, from another century, from another place and in a language
not our own is of greatest moment. The existentialist retorts that
nothing is more important than the situation and people of the
here and now, no matter how petty or meaningless they be in broad
terms, simply because they say that this is all we really have.

378.
The burden of these thoughts, these ideas, these feelings is
often too onerous to have the strength to treat them seriously.
Nevertheless there is truth in the madman's laughter as well.

379.
"When you got nothing, you got nothing to lose"—and
this could either be the nihilist or hedonist anthem of
iconoclasm or it could be the starting point of a hopeful
spirit to whom even the simplest thing brings great joy.

380.
On the surface all appears tranquil, but what lies beneath is
a turmoil and maelstrom that brews ever stronger and more
sinister. Once again, the world will hold its breath . . .

381.
Women have a way of turning themselves to stone,
like a marble sculpture standing in a sepulcher.

382.
Democracy implies moral and aesthetic relativism.

383.
Pity, wrongly felt, turns humans into animals.

384.
If God is truly as beautiful and glorious as they say, it would
seem he would not want cowering imbeciles for followers.

385.
"A woman's power lies in her sex; a man's power is in resisting sex."

386.
Does the artist have a moral obligation to create *beautiful* things?

387.
Egalitarianism is holding the world in a tense civility.

388.

Communism is the collective Will to Power of the lower men.

389.

"Mark my words: Spanish influenza, it's coming back."

390.

The lower men piss away their lives but often not even in such a human thing as over-indulgence in alcohol. The drunkard knows of his discontent and turns to the bottle. The contentedness of the lower men is nauseating, as are his civil niceties, laziness, fatness, lack of zeal, and all these under the pretense of responsibility.

391.

One of the things that sickens me the most of all about the Christians is that they will buy all sorts of consumer goods, made in oppressive circumstances, have far too much of everything, then, when some "church" decides to do a "mission" trip to Honduras for a week, they pack up all their second-hand crap and send it back to the people who made it—and they call it charity.

392.

We laugh at death because we fear it so much.

393.

Before the modern age there was a vocation for myopics in the absence of lenses: chanting, praying, copying and illuminating manuscripts, none requiring great powers of far sight. Now the same of the would-be religious sit in cubicles and stare at electro-screens all day and manipulate a blasé binary world. Perhaps there are more than "10" types of people in the world, however.

394.

"Most vices I can change, but one seems insurmountable: being always pensive."

395.

One might ask which is more important: happiness or greatness. The Germanics of old would have responded: what's the difference?

396.

All we have left of Solon of Athens is a few poetic fragments;
while Wordsworth purposely composed the same.

397.

No matter how beautiful you are at this moment,
you will someday die. If then at this moment you are
beautiful, enjoy it fully, for someday you will die.

398.

"Otto Weininger was right!" (or was he?)

399.

A valiant few are fighting tooth and nail to keep the American society
afloat, from sliding into utter decadence and then destruction. I say
let it fall, and we shall build something more glorious thing upon the
skeletons and ruins, or we at least have learned the price of decadence.

400.

"I would be much more troubled about the travails of this
physical universe were I convinced of its actual existence."

401.

"Yes, I keep a revolver under my pillow, because
it's always nice to have the option."

402.

"God, sex, suicide." It was not too long ago that we used to talk
seriously, or at least passionately, about the weighty issues of life.
Now that God is dead, sex is trivial and suicide is just another
among many options, does anything in life have meaning? (And
yes, I know Camus addresses these but his answer must not have
inspired because I do not recall his solution to these problems.)

403.

It is certain that we are amusing ourselves to death,
but what *fun* we are having in the process!

404.

If Freud were right, and the sublimation of our primitive
drives due to repression by society is the font of culture, it
should then come as no surprise that now, when there is hardly
any repression, that there should be a cultural vacuum.

405.

The lack of sacramentalism in most forms of Protestantism had lead
to a Philistinism in their thoughts (or lack thereof) on aesthetics, for
if the physical elements of bread and wine are not imbued with some
spiritual force in themselves then it remains that we must ascend to
the world of spirit, thus making physicality an afterthought. Therefore,
it does not matter if their churches are ugly and irresponsible in so
many ways, for matter counts for nothing; only spirit is important,
and this is infinitely separated from the physical world.

406.

Sophocles was both a soldier and laurel crowned playwright. His
younger contemporary Thucydides was both historian and general.
Marcus Aurelius was not only the last of the good emperors, he wrote
a rather serious treatise on Stoic philosophy. David and Achilles both
played harp and sang in addition to being the greatest champions of their
age. Men are capable of greatness in multiple spheres simultaneously.
In the present age though, men are discouraged from these ends. For
to see one great at many things, not the specialist, would be to be
reminded of our own laziness, pettiness, lowness, and decadence.

407.

Usque ad venturum Regis.

408.

Smashing idols was once a sort of glorious iconoclastic past-time
of the *avant garde* philosophers. Now one does not even need a
hammer as the idols of our day are so small and paltry that a good
stomp of the foot will do. However, these little gods are all too
ubiquitous to smash them all, no matter how hard one tries.

409.
"Just because I cannot save the world, does not mean that
I may stand idly by and watch it fall to pieces."

410.
Love of what is good often looks like an over-arching hatred of
everything whatsoever when the world is in such a sorry state of affairs.

411.
Even the deepest sorrows, through love, may be
sublimated into something beautiful.

412.
It is easy to think on those who will live forever, Dante, St.
Anselm, Constantine, but it is hard and painful to think on those
who will perhaps be forever dead: mothers, brothers, sons.

413.
Every man, in addition to doing penance for his own sins, over
the course of his life will have to cover over a multitude of the sins
of others. It is only by love and will that he shall achieve this.

414.
Love is the font of all Will, though it be at times veiled
by the harsh and silent masculine façade.

415.
Once men strove with the gods and it made them glorious and
heroic, if sometimes tragic. So how is it then that they have so
easily succumbed to being ruled by inanimate machines?

416.
It seems that in the present age wealth is based on position of
advantage in a vast pyramid-scheme, which in turn is based mostly on
imaginary money. It was once that men counted themselves wealthy
in herds of cattle, healthy sons and the strength of their right hand.

417.
"I agree with myself."—a tautology so obvious, and yet so
few are courageous enough to vocalize this claim.

418.
To be a Christian is nothing more than to be truly
human, rightly defined. None who refuse to be good
humans then may call themselves Christians.

419.
I love smashing the machines, for in that destructive glory I
remind myself that I am not cold and mechanical, that I am even
on occasion irrational. It reminds me that I am, rather, human.

420.
It is impossible for a poet to lie and to remain a good poet.

421.
These walnuts lying on the ground alongside these city streets
and in their parks are like little bags of potato chips that the
rich and poor alike refuse to bend down to pick up and eat.

422.
All our greatest ideas and feelings come to us in dreams,
yet they die, sadly before the dawn of morning light.

423.
A scribble of ink on a scrap of paper, dry and crumpled with age, yet
who among us could estimate the infinite value of a great Idea?

424.
To achieve enlightenment and remember it, and ecstasy in
absence of alcohol or narcotics; this is the power and genius of
the meditative religious. I confess that I am not their equal.

425.

We Americans do not believe in anything, at least not very strongly.
This is why we are horrified at those who believe even unto death, who
might even challenge us and bring death upon us. We are horrified
at this because if we are called upon to die without belief in anything,
then our death is not only worthless, it is also meaningless. Yet a few
hundred true believers hold the whole world hostage with baited breath.

426.

Do not cast your pearls amongst swine, neither waste your
best and most beautiful emotions on paltry subjects.

427.

The early modern Dutch are the classic example of a bare Calvinism
at work thoroughly through an entire culture: the relinquishing of
religious images and liturgy; the build-up of capital through Spartan
lifestyle; the use the seas for commerce, and colonies for trade only,
not the expansion of their nation or religion. Only the Dutch were
allowed into Japan because they did not proselytize. The final result
of this utter separation of religion from the rest of culture has had the
sad result of the current moral bankruptcy of the Netherlands and the
imminent collapse of their nation under the weight of sturdy Muslim
immigrants. Yet their business schools are still full of students, while
their few Catholics and farmers have emigrated to North America.

428.

"Why am I the only one who realizes how awesome I am?"
—if his excellence be true, is the self-acknowledgement of it still *hubris*?

429.

Poetry gives strength to language, as do sermons and orations
to a lesser extent. Prose, as it tries to mimic colloquial speech, or
convey information without bothering with beauty, is the primary
source of language degeneration. Thus no language, and by easy
extrapolation, no culture can long survive without poetry.

430.
All philosophers, poets, theologians, warriors, kings and emperors—all great men must have a worthy opponent against whom they may exercise their greatness. Achilles and Hector, Kant and Hume, Napoleon and Wellington, Nietzsche and Socrates, great men would, in the absence of a rival, simply weep.

431.
It is perhaps true that the Americans are truly no worse than any of the others. The only difference is that Americans have not even the vestiges of folk culture standing under them and giving somewhat a foundation, a *raison d'etre* that is the birthright of most people in most places. Thus our folly and stupidity is all the more ridiculous because it is so transparent and not even dressed up in the garb of folk custom. *Kyrie Eleison!*

432.
"As a Christian, every morning I awake and decide whether I will accept Christ or reject him, whether I will strive to do good, or allow evil desire to overcome me. The true Christian is the one who has the seated habit of saying yes to Christ more than saying no. It is the same with love, with virtue, with anything good; we make the choice each day what kind of person we will be."

433.
Success is a category by which I do not at all measure my life. It is as empty as the bankrolls of those in the grave.

434.
Hugo von Hofmannsthal was close, closer than anyone I have ever known. I have that feeling again, of tears, of Being, of impulse and taking hold, like I could almost leap into a world of completely reconciled finitude, infinity and consciousness. I feel so close to it that it tingles through my bones and causes my heart to ache.

435.

My flair for the theatrical does not make me less genuine a
human but rather more, for there is something in our very
human-ness that is caught up in the stage and the theater. Let
us then be good players—which is to say take our role seriously
(that would include playing the fool with gusto). Let us play
with passion, avoid apathy and spectatorship, for we all shall
have to make our final exit regardless of how we played.

436.
"Öd und leer das Meer . . ."

T.S. Eliot likely sat with a fat book of quotes next to him while writing
poetry, but he still knew which ones to insert at the exact right place.

437.

The difference between a man who is rightfully confident and the one
who is overbearing is defined by this: how physically attractive he is.

438.

Form and structure, rather than limiting our freedom is the
only place within which true freedom can flourish.

439.

The love of a man and a woman can only flourish within the bounds of
respect, restraint, openness to new creations, and true passion for the
other that results in new life, which is always the overflow of love.

440.

We are horrified by the thought of utter randomness and also of
determinism. The former makes us feel meaningless, and the latter
causes the same because it turns humanity into the machine. It is that
thin line between the extremes where humanity must strive to remain.
This principle applies most of all perhaps to the aesthetics of life.

441.

Virtue is doing right when no one is looking; virtue is doing right
for its own sake; virtue is doing right when one is weak, weary
and barely able to stand, when one could so easily fall into vice.

442.
Not grammar, but poetry is the ground upon which all language is based.

443.
Language connected to poetry, music, drama, i.e. action—strong beautiful
action, without which the culture and society will languish and decay.

444.
Language, language, language—we are playing language games
to be sure, but let our games be beautiful, theatric and true. Mr.
Wittgenstein, meet Friedrich Nietzsche and Hugo von Hofmannsthal.

445.
We still fear the Germans, not only for their past militarism, but more
so, we find their truths difficult concerning world, consciousness, idea,
culture, art and society. We are more content in our bland mediocrity,
slumping toward extinction. As an example, Goethe is perhaps the
most important European *vir omnium scientiarum* since Milton, and
perhaps even since Dante, yet who among us has read his works?

446.
Inspiration may be hard to come by these days; the standard has been
raised high, but when she comes, it is like drops of gold, sweet as honey.

447.
If Protestantism fulfilled the human lust for utter simplicity
in religious expression, for national identity and for money
(with its incipient capitalism), then Islam fulfilled the same
desire for this simplicity and combined it with an imposed,
almost unnatural austerity and religious conformity.

448.
To refuse to play the music of Wagner or Lizst due to their
supposed anti-semitism is the moral equivalent of refusing to play
Tchaikovsky because of his homosexuality. Ah, the moral hypocrisy
of the majority! They *absolutize* as much as anyone ever has but
do it with a *faux* smile in the name of tolerance and equality.

449.
"Great wits are sure to madness near allied,
And thin partitions do their bounds divide."
—A thing written in verse does not merely
seem more true; it *is* more true.

450.
"You said that you were in a non-suicidal despair,
so I just figured it was Presbyterian."
(a friend referring to my stint at the Protestant seminary)

451.
"I have yearned for love so long and so deeply that it nearly breaks my
heart. But I also have been afraid of it, sneered at it, shunned it and fallen
in love with the idea of it. I am no longer in denial; I am man enough to
admit my need and my weakness—which is the most beautiful of all."

452.
An aphorism, a poem, a feeling—inspired by strong drink: Was it our
most true self coming out from behind the veil? Or was it a foreign,
false and fleeting Muse, who flew away with the dawn of morning?

453.
The entire *oeuvre* of my short stories was written under the
influence of that wretched national brand of Argentine beer.
That, sadly, tells me more about the stories than the stories
themselves. Never under-estimate the importance of the
external trappings when it comes to the creative process!

454.
"You are all taking yourselves too seriously!" (written in a black-leather
notebook, by a lone figure in a hipster bar, while smoking a
clove cigarette, who was working on a book of aphorisms)

455.
"One of the greatest desires of my life has been to experience an
authentic culture; it has not yet happened." (Wm. Verlander)

456.

Both art and artifact belong in public space; it were better to have
the city square adorned with sculpture of its heroes than the private
home with paintings. The taste of the community, more than the
individual ought to be indulged (if it be good taste, rather). But since
there is no longer common culture or taste, no public monument can
have universal appeal but will generally be offensive to some group or
another, or be so pathetically neutral as to lose all aesthetic force. Alas!

457.

The mass-man may be our reality and our fate, but
need we celebrate him so exuberantly?

458.

True taste and maturity in artistic production stunted, now the juvenile
and adult produce the same banal *oeuvre*, but the youth is forgiven
for his naivety while the adult is a culpable agent in ugliness.

459.

After we have destroyed all that is good, beautiful and heroic, what then?

460.

"I do not understand this art"—art is not meant to be
cognitively understood, at least not primarily. "I am not
moved by it."—that is the important sentiment.

461.

The cream always rises to the top, but hopefully
it has not curdled by the time it does so.

462.

The artist must reflect the taste of the *Volk*, but also must inspire
the same to more sublime heights of aesthetic enjoyment. He
must give us thoughts and feelings we never imagined we had,
yet were still deeply our own without yet knowing it.

463.

We walk into the cliché haunt of the frat-boy college bar.
He leans over to me and says: "Why would I want to look
at any of these pie-faced mannequins?" We walk out.

464.

I once thought my ideas, quips, and aphorisms to be witty,
clever and profound. Upon reading von Hofmannsthal, I found
out that I was an unwitting world-soul plagiarist. Thankfully
few read the German these days, so I will keep my claim to
cleverness but only with tongue firmly planted in cheek.

465.

To say that a thing of beauty is a joy forever presumes several
other truths: the eternity of the soul which perceives and
yearns for beauty; the capacity to apprehend true beauty,
and the eternity of beauty as an eternal category.

466.

Music—rather than celebrating our decadence, folly, vice, or
worse—justifying it, music should rather confirm or encourage
the best parts of us—love, courage, sacrifice, true sentiment, even
greatness. Music reflects and defines culture in so many ways. If
our music be wretched how shall we ever have any higher men?

467.

"Just because I take nothing seriously in this society, does
not mean I take nothing seriously categorically."

468.

It is certain that we are amusing ourselves to death. Ah, but
what fun we are having in the process! Do you not see with
what rapt pleasure they gaze at their various telescreens?

469.

"Arthur Schopenhauer changed my life."—ah,
but who is to say for the better?

470.

I still consider German Idealism to be *avant-garde* when
it comes to philosophy. It is still, rather, the last serious
attempt at philosophy undertaken in the West.

471.

What is the end of any idea, any truth, any profound insight unless
it can reach down to the level of the *Volk*? I would not be a useless
academician, but rather one who stands up and plays the game.

472.

Was ist männlich? (What is manly?). The new, higher, true
redefining of manliness (and specifically *not* its negation)
will be the preface to the rebirth of culture.

473.

In the late 19th century, at the new Walnut Street-style penitentiary
at Faustenburg, the Bibles for solitary inmates were replaced
with Schopenhauer's "World as Will and Representaion."
Within a month each one of the inmates had committed
suicide and the state had rid itself of its social burden and
arguably created its finest philosophers in one fell swoop.

474.

Anyone who begins to think will arrive, but those
who think rightly will arrive more quickly.

475.

Once upon a time . . . my soul was very beautiful, and very sad.

476.

The refusal to eat and enjoy delicious food and wine is a moral
deficiency; the scorning of beautiful music and poetry a spiritual one.

477.

To hate one's culture, history and place is, quite simply, to hate one's very own self. However, these self-haters, because of their lack of ability to appreciate and feel the epic of their own race, history and culture, are the same ones who are too weak to turn a violent hand toward themselves and change their lives, despite their self-loathing.

478.

For most of us it is not really a lack of knowledge; rational free agents do, after all, have the capacity to arrive at many truths by actually thinking. No! For the vast majority it is not ignorance that holds us back but a lack of will. Comfort of lifestyle leads to an impotence in the fight against the most obvious stupidity, falsity and injustice of the machine—and all only because our bellies are too full!

479.

For those who neither desire knowledge, nor have passion to discover truth, why do we expend immense amounts of time and money "educating" them for decades? Simply this: control. The expediency of the State demands many faithful automatons. The State however, more often than not, has been the enemy of Truth and *Kultur*.

480.

Systems rarely evolve or change for the better. Rather they wear out, grow old and die. They are then cast aside by bold creators of the New.

481.

In the absence of transcendent Religion or of *Kultur* it is hard to imagine why the great number of men bother to remain alive. Their self-destructive addictions and habits manifest their apathy and love of death; their remaining in the world affirms the goodness of life in spite of themselves.

482.

Do ideas beget actions or actions ideas? There is a third possibility; ideas are actions and actions in fact are ideas.

483.

Beauty, Truth, Goodness, Virtue, Culture, Ideas, Art, Music:
what does it mean to pursue these in the every day? There
is, or ought to be, a presupposed *Weltanschauung*

484.

There is no longer any middle ground, though many are refusing
to take sides. Solon would have cast them out of the *polis*. But I
do not have the normal political divide in mind, but something
far more fundamental: those who believe in human culture, and
those who are the enemies of all truth and beauty in us.

485.

For now they may be strong, but those who believe in nothing
at all, the politicos and profiteers will soon have their masks torn
away and their weakness revealed. One poor man with an honest
skill is in fact more powerful than the president of the world, for
their power is an illusion and not based on anything real. They have
deluded the simpletons long enough. One leader, who could exhibit
a real skill in something, anything, could topple the whole house
of cards with the swing of a hammer. He is the man who not only
can use language with good rhetoric, but who can build a house,
plow a field, brew beer, play music and write a poem. In short,
one true human could overcome all the machines combined.

486.

Wagner, the last gasp of Western culture, but the glorious
death throes were just how he would have wanted . . .

487.

Any criterion other than genius is not worth having.

488.

Reading a bad book is morally worse than watching
television, for television, at least, is intuitively known to be
meaningless, not to be taken seriously, but the very act of
reading might trick the mind and heart into taking all too
seriously the pop-trash novel, the pseudo-philosophy, and
the banal histories of the things of no great moment.

489.

The difference between cynicism and jollity is the ability to laugh in genuine joy, rather than sneer at the present age.

490.

Bar scene: The music was as mediocre as the beer, yet a great crowd had gathered. In search of true human culture perhaps? The clientele was as cliché as an American novel—doughy, non-virile men, and women clearly lacking self-confidence . . .

491.

I doubt the Americans' abilities to make good decisions and sound value judgments, even in the absence of alcohol.

492.

The music ended too soon, and instead of sublimation, instead of longing, we were left with only a hunger for French Fries.

493.

C'est terrible, c'est terrible, c'est terrible! A Quebecois visits the United States.

494.

We found gold; we had slaves; we feared no evil; we trans-valued all values; we were born into utter luxury—and yet we boast.

495.

Trust no man who speaks before he has suffered.

496.

Life=theater

497.

Actions 9/10; Words 1/10

498.

The question about every act of art or culture that the artist, observer and participant must ask: would my life and the lives of others be impoverished without it? If the answer is no, it were better left undone. This is the standard of all creativity artistic and otherwise.

499.

Being a clever cynic does not necessarily negate the existence of an immortal soul, and being such shall certainly never save the same.

500.

"Once I had time to feel beautifully, to think, to enjoy both sorrow and exultation. That did not help the system in any way, so they turned me into a machine and made me quite productive. Now I feel nothing at all."

501.

Some may claim it is decadent to lie in the dark and listen to sad music, to let yourself feel it fully. I am not sure it is any better to be so busy as to be distracted from all possible sadness; I am sure the latter is less human.

502.

Once had I been told that ideas have consequences and that words in fact are a form of action; this seemed to me nearly intuitive and certainly true and good. Then I went to university for graduate studies . . .

503.

Nothing has touched the soul so deeply as music; none so truly or purely as the Gregorian chants at a Latin Mass.

504.

Religious devotion must always seem insane to the materialist; the inverse is equally true.

505.

The highest words are those that do not merely describe the action, but in fact achieve the action itself. Very few examples come to mind.

506.

There seems to me little difference (except difference of importance perhaps) between the cult of the saints, the cult of dead heroes, and the obsession with long gone writers who are studied in the university with a deveteé-like obsession. These last ones though are false in their claim of being scientific and impersonal. No human could ever thus be interested in anything living or dead.

507.

It does not seem any less plausible that the dead live on after
their body is lifeless than that the moment of death extinguishes
all individual existence, and the universe with it.

508.

It does not trouble me greatly to throw all human states,
faculties, systems and otherwise into the category of
construct—for in doing so we again can establish the two
most important categories of all: faith and beauty.

509.

Belief, true faith, can never be based on a purely intellectual
understanding because I can very easily admit a "truth" in my
intellect without being in any way in intimate contact with
it; action only can result from faith. On the other hand one
might argue that true understanding of a thing means intimacy
with it. Having the proper affection for something means both
understanding it and loving it; these two may in fact be the
same thing. And the modern dichotomy between these two is an
instance of the unhelpful fractioning of the human psyche.

510.

Language as concealing: Language as revealing: Both as servants of truth.

511.

Freedom of art means a joyful conformity to Nature and Truth,
being able to bring all aspects of these into a flourishing health.

512.

Fluctuation of the Self?

513.

From whom shall I learn? I am too old to be an apprentice, only
too old when I compare myself with the living; the blissfully
dead of the centuries are quite old enough to be my masters.

514.

Natura not nature. *Physis* not physics.

515.

So, since we have no integrated culture in modern society, no common
ground, no religion, no music or even a common morality, both
our social mores and even language disintegrates. Thus we build
micro-cliques where we feel comfortable, isolated within a single society,
utterly limited in our perspective, despite the cries of multi-culturalism.
To ever understand another we must first understand ourselves, but we
in the west are a shell; we have no "self" left because we have no "us."

516.

Conflict between social obligation and personal fulfillment is
not a *necessary* state of affairs. If both society and individual
were devoted to pursuing the Good, no conflict would
exist, except the constant striving toward said Good.

517.

We need more of our best minds pursuing beauty and
greatness and fewer trying to build a mountain of money.

518.

The (former?) United States is the only country in the world that
I know of, where the impoverished are fatter than French kings.
Everywhere else poverty means not having enough food to eat. Yet
they cry out in lament while the rest of the world suffers due to the
consumerism and decadence of the so-called American poor!

519.

"Wagner, if you were alive, would we be enemies or steadfast friends?"

520.

The ideas of tragedy, sorrow, melancholy, presuppose
truth, beauty and goodness—lost of course. Otherwise
whence should come the cause of our sadness?

521.

If Oswald Spengler were alive today I would challenge
him to a fist-fight, except that I am afraid he would revel
in it and chide from his broken jaw: "I told you so."

522.

To the true artist, not the degenerate pretender, each act of living
takes on an aesthetic and theatrical quality based in truth. Every
gulp of wine, every wince of pain, every gesture of ecstasy . . . He
is more human than us all in his triumph and despair, but
by becoming his followers we truly become ourselves.

523.

Sitting there, across the way, late-night espresso or glass of absinthe:
Object of *your* contemplation. If any more morose
I would take you for a French novelist.

524.

Imagine fighting an entire war, sending the youth to their grim death,
bombing civilians and true cultures just to prove that there is nothing
beautiful, nothing higher, nothing worth living and dying for—yet
democracies have fought wars, both within and without, for well over
a century based on just such a premise. They shall have their reward.

525.

"America" as deliberate anti-culture State—founded on reason,
not spirit and pre-eminent among modern "Civilizations."

526.

Some destroy culture out of the sheer joy of power that comes
from toppling a seemingly immovable object, that, and the joy of
the knife, that spills the blood of all things beautiful; others mean
well, believe they are doing a thing for the betterment of mankind,
but in their folly and ignorance also open the door for the roaring
lion, who prowls through the world seeking the ruin of souls.

527.

The words a man hears, how he chooses to speak (both manner
and content), his attention to beauty in all its forms, the careful
nurture of lofty thoughts and sentiments—all these will, in
the end, define his very Being. If I choose degradation and
ugliness, my soul will soon reflect this choice, if beauty, then the
contrary. To paraphrase Erasmus: *humani facti, non nati sunt.*

528.

It is perhaps too easy to say goodbye, to walk away and enjoy the sweet and beautiful melancholy, thinking what might have been. To remain with the beloved for all times requires strong will and commitment, and much hardship as well. But from this all true joy springs.

529.

Once, in an age of time, there arises from the hazy mists of obscurity a hero of words: a Poet. He is one who gives language its voice, and the people theirs through it, who endues once more a sense of meaning and power in the Word, as if it had not been "chattered to death" by the countless millions. He is an uncommon hero, but after he speaks, we hold more firmly, more beautifully, our tenuous grip on life, on ourselves, on the universe.

530.

I once thought that with age the intense sadness would cease, or at least lessen. Rather, it has intensified with the years so that a single line of poetry, a single sentiment, a single moment brought to recollection is like a razor-sharp dagger of ice. The difference is this: I now know the name and truth of that pain-filled longing—it is called Joy.

531.

Those who believe nothing achieve nothing:
welcome to the world's impasse.

532.

I have yet to find a word that could be considered an antonym for degeneracy. It is more a feeling of the Good than a definition as such, but perhaps we lack this word because when degeneracy is *not* happening in society there is little reason to critique; the Good simply *is* and does not need an epithet.

533.

For the amount of luxury to be present in a society that even allows for decadence, somewhere, someone must be enslaved. Yet we remain shameless consumerists.

534.
Why is it that once upon a time the most important centers of a culture, society or nation were once filled with beautiful palaces, lofty churches or temples, noble town homes, theatres, halls, and parks—in short, inspiring and lovely places and buildings? And now the main centers, though a token or façade of beauty is sometimes present, are the ugliest, most wretched and demoralizing of all? Is this to be our legacy to the generations? How will they not rejoice then at our downfall?

535.
True friendship is timeless; it recognizes no limits of time and space.

536.
The same sadness that often leads to beauty can metamorphose into desperate depression whence only ugliness comes.

537.
So many images of ourselves have we contrived, that we only vaguely recognize the face that confronts us in the mirror.

538.
Finitude: there is no word more sadly stark. Yet only those who fight and strive against it shall overcome.

539.
"I will not be ashamed for being strong, for being beautiful, intelligent, for being excellent." Ah, but does not their writing of such *apologia* betray an insecurity and shame at being such things in the face of the nihilistic masses?

540.
Revolutionaries rarely start out as such. They begin, rather, as the great Idealists of humanity, even pacifist, but always overly optimistic that once the masses get a taste of truth they will run in joyful bliss into the arms of the new system, a system that will bind men together in peace and cooperation. This necessarily failing, they then grow bitter, weary of the impasse, smash the walls and try to bring light into the cave, rather than bring those in the cave out into the light. Yet one can never make to see those who would remain blind.

541.
Aeneas and Abraham: wanderers, warriors,
sojourners, and founders—True Believers.

542.
"I long for you and yearn to gather up the pieces of your tattered soul,
like no other, for mine as well, is likewise torn from life's travail."

543.
The only things in life worth anything are those that make you cry.

544.
"At this rate, I will never become Holy Roman
Emperor." He said after a week of indolence, indulging
in a binge of reading degenerate philosophy.

545.
Melancholy, in fact, can sometimes be hilarious—usually not though . . .

546.
Humility, if it is truly to be a virtue, must be something more than
contentment and apology for being a rather pathetic human specimen.

547.
Misery of the soul is also a hidden hope and blessing. For it shows
that somewhere, perhaps deeply damaged and buried beneath ruins
and ashes, that there is a soul badly shaken, but more or less intact
and functioning as a soul should—crying out to take us higher.

548.

Alexander, Caesar, and Napoleon: conquerors; Plato, St. Thomas, Schopenhauer: philosophers; Newton, Heisenberg, Einstein: scientists. My mind fails to think of even one, let alone three, "great" businessmen. This is because greatness is a category not allowed to the shop keeper; he is *per definitionem* petty. (Students, notice the use of *per* with the accusative!). Since greatness is a species of virtue, is it any wonder then, that in a world run by accountants, imaginary currencies and greed greater than any Shylock, that virtue could be neither found, nor even named? Yet the Christians (many at least) preach cut-throat capitalism as if it were a system that not only could, but necessarily does lead to godliness. Our powers of thought have apparently failed us in the wake of cheap electrode slaves, commuter-tanks and frozen chocolate-covered waffles.

549.

Is anything so coldly calculating as the mind of a woman? Is anything capable of greater purity and simple truth? As Socrates taught us: the potential for great good means potential for great evil as well.

550.

Thesis: The aversion and derision of the grotesque in folk tale, myth and literature shows the biological underpinning of aversion among humanity toward genetic monstrosity as exemplars lacking fitness.

551.

Imagine what greater heights of culture the Greeks would have achieved if they had better sublimated their sex drive rather than squandering their energies on pederasty.

552.

Anti-Socratics: Tactics for avoiding the examined life: mindless entertainments; political "activism;" quietism/Stoicism; work-aholism.

553.

The "swerve" of Lucretius, where the strict cause and effect of the cosmos seems to hold its breath a moment, no matter how rare or short-lived—this is the realm of all will and creativity, in short, all that is meaningful and truly human.

554.

The present age "pop culture" music, from below, is just as artificial
as the French courtly culture of the 18th century was from above.
They are artificial; that does not mean in no way good, strictly
speaking; it simply means they are no true expression of the folk.
If these artificial expressions extinguish the natural and organic
folk culture they inevitably will bring about their own destruction
as well, as in the purges of the Revolution. The replacements,
if equally unnatural, will repeat the cycles of blood. We wait
with baited breath (we are doing this much these days) . . .

555.

A thing as beautiful and tragic as the *Deutscher Geist* can never be bandied
about among the many, thrown to the winds in a mass-movement.
This is the fatal flaw of Nazism, and we have seen its outcomes; a
world afraid to believe in any beauty or culture whatsoever, a world
afraid to believe in itself because it fears its own awful potential.

556.

The evil of capitalism lies not primarily in its need for a throng
of low-cost, rock-bottom wage workers; there has always been
and will be a lower class of proletarians and hirelings in any
society. Rather, its greatest evil is this: the only motivation in the
whole system is profit, neither virtue, nor honor. So in the end
the "normal" person in capitalism takes no action, no thought for
anything except profit. Yet the greatest acts for a human are those
in which profit takes little or no part. Rather pursue glory than
profit! It is loftier and more humane. A king could be a hero or a
tyrant; the entrepreneur will be judged by the bottom line of the
ledger. (This is so oft been said, but we have yet to learn it.)

557.

Most academic departments found in the modern university did not even
exist as areas of study until the decline and death of Western culture.

558.

Philosophy does not need the epithet "continental." What the
Anglophones do could be considered more like parlor tricks and
word games than serious philosophy. (Yet I write in English . . .)

559.
Museums—as has been said before, those vast and oft too
cheerful or too banal sepulchers of culture; yet the collection
which is truly momentous, like the grave of a great man, still
bring me to tears, remembering what we once were and did.

560.
It somehow seems appropriate for genius to die young;
they are too much for the world: Shelley, Raphael,
Alexander. And yet Goethe lived unto a ripe old age.

561.
The nearly inherent melancholy and depression of the
Calvinist Protestants: a religio-race-consciousness?

562.
Omar Khayyam is even more nihilistic, though less heroic,
than the most Nordic of northern mythologies, and yet his
tone is almost cheerful. Is the sun simply that strong of an
emotional mentor? Or is there some lack of profundity among
those who can no longer even weep at the idea of finitude?

563.
These gentlemen's games, are they veils for cowardice or
aggression? That they are veils, this is beyond doubt.

564.
Those drives you feel so strongly, like forces drive the cosmos. Wait
but a moment, gaze deep, breathe and meditate a moment on true
ends; they will become a deeper and a more beautiful force indeed.
The same gulp of wine that brings us to overcoming ourselves, often
achieves the opposite among those who would deny its *essence*.

565.
There is more virtue in one swing of the hammer or slash
of the sword than a thousand strokes of the pen, if and only
if these former motions be devoted to creating beauty.

566.

We have every kind of excess, except for any of the right ones.

567.

Ennui: the curse of those who do not complete their quest in virtue.

568.

I have as many friends as men in the world, if they truly be men.

569.

The lust to live, survive, to exist may be quite strong, too
strong among the many. The desire to live well, to truly
live is found only among the few. There will always be
more robbers and riff-raff than martyrs or saints.

570.

Culture is what happens when a people have both freedom to
create and also love of beauty and virtue, enough at least to create
in reflection of the Good. Otherwise freedom becomes merely
a pretense for abuse, ugliness and ultimately, destruction.

571.

Prometheus chained to the rock of the Caucasus, and Apollo captured—
darkness. The night of Dionysus, which began in a joyful bacchanal has
become the horror of nakedness; alone in a cruel throng of madmen . . .

DEUTSCHES ADDENDUM

(The following semi-quips were originally thought by the
author in German; it seemed best to leave them un-translated:
All this took place under the influence of megalomania.)

I.
Gleich Wasser kam ich; gleich dem Wind, ich gehe.

II.
Diese Schwierigkeiten sind auch nur Teilnehmer
der Welt der Vorstellungen.

III.
Die jetzige Krise ist so gross wie der Zwerg von gestern.

IV.
Nicht ohne, aber durch die richtige Empfindsamkeit überwinden.

V.
Sie sind so schwach wie ohnmächtige Körper, und wir
nennen sie Helden; willkommen in der jetzigen Zeit.

VI.
Unser höheres Leben und unsere besten Ideen kommen in der Zeit des
Schlafens. Die Träume sind geistliche Wesen die durch empfindsame
Seelen fliegen. Nicht ohne Vernunft sondern jenseits derselben—deren
Diener sie ist, nicht Meister. Wenn wir diese zwei getrennten Dinge
statt sie zu unterscheiden, zusammenbringen, werden wir denn
nicht mehr zerspaltete sondern vollkommene wahre Menschen.

VII.
Gott is gewaltätig und stürmisch—ja, aber auch gut.

VIII.
Nicht alle Gedichte haben Wörter; die Besten haben keine.

IX.

Wie oft ist Größe zwischen uns hindurchgelaufen, aber wir wussten
es nicht, nur empfanden wir das vage Gefühl unserer eigenen
Kleinigkeit und dann ist es gleich wieder verschwunden.

X.

Der, der fürchtet, ist schon tot. Nur der Mann der
freiwillig sterben kann, ist noch am Leben.

XI.

Keinen Zweck haben, heißt keine Lebensbedeutung. Ohne Kultur
kann es keinen Zweck geben. Deshalb das jetztige Unbehagen.

XII.

Der Traum ist vorbei; er war aber immer nur Scheingold
(über die Vereinigten Staaten gesprochen)

XIII.

Die Welt ist klein und kleinartig geworden.

XIV.

"Der Tod ist der seligste Traum." Das stimmt aber nur für die Heiligen.

XV.

Die Verfluchung des Reichtums ist nämlich
kein menschliches Leben zu erfahren.

XVI.

Die Vereinigten Staaten, sowie Athen: Freiheit
wegen der Sklaverei der Anderen.

XVII.

Dichter, Philosophen und Betrunkene schreiben
auf Deutsch—komisch, oder?

XVIII.

Das zerbrochene Herz: Vorspiel zum Wille.

XIX.
Ich warte auf nichts mehr als Begeisterung.

XX.
Jetzt geht es um Sprachreinigung.

Printed in the United States
By Bookmasters